NAHUM
Meet the True God

Richard Caldwell

KRESS
BIBLICAL
RESOURCES

Published by:
Kress Biblical Resources
www.kressbiblical.com

Unless otherwise indicated, all scripture quotations are from the ESV® Bible (The Holy Bible, English Standard Version®), copyright © 2001 by Crossway, a publishing ministry of Good News Publishers. Used by permission. All rights reserved.

NASB: Scripture quotations taken from the New American Standard Bible® (NASB), Copyright © 1960, 1962, 1963, 1968, 1971, 1972, 1973,1975, 1977, 1995 by The Lockman Foundation. Used by permission. www.Lockman.org

NIV: Scripture taken from the Holy Bible, NEW INTERNATIONAL VERSION®, NIV® Copyright © 1973, 1978, 1984, 2011 by Biblica, Inc.® Used by permission. All rights reserved worldwide.

ISBN: 978-1-934952-30-6

DEDICATION

To all my brothers in the ministry who tirelessly labor on behalf of Christ and His sheep.

CONTENTS

ACKNOWLEDGMENTS

I would like to thank Nathan Ramirez for his help with reading and editing. He's a faithful pastor and a treasured son-in-law. Additional thanks to Jim and Gail Swindle for their editing work. I would also like to thank my good friend Rick Kress for his help in formatting this volume. He is a faithful friend and a servant of Christ who works to get the truth of God's Word into the hands of needy people.

1
MEET THE TRUE GOD
(1:1)

If we wish to be skillful and faithful evangelists to "our time," then there's something we must be fully aware of. In our time we are not simply declaring the truth about God to a world that does not know Him. We are attempting to declare the truth about God to a world that thinks it already knows about Him.

That is, we are not just engaging in an information campaign as we seek to declare biblical truth; we are fighting against a satanically inspired misinformation campaign.

When Paul stood in the Areopagus and declared the "unknown God" to the Athenians, those people acknowledged that Paul's God was unknown to them. They acknowledged their ignorance of what Paul was preaching.

Acts 17:19 And they took him and brought him to the Areopagus, saying, "May we know what this new teaching is that you are presenting? 20 For you bring some strange things to our ears. We wish to know therefore what these things mean." 21 Now all the Athenians and the foreigners who lived there would spend their time in nothing except telling or hearing something new. 22 So Paul, standing in the midst of the Areopagus, said: "Men of Athens, I perceive that in every way you are very religious. 23 For as I passed along and observed the objects of your worship, I found also an altar with this inscription, 'To the unknown god.' What therefore you worship as unknown, this I proclaim to you.

We, on the other hand, declare the God of the Bible, in the United States, to a culture that thinks it understands Christianity. In truth, it doesn't. Ours is a very syncretistic culture. The God of Christianity, assumed in the current cultural milieu, is a mixture of what the Bible says, and what the current moral condition wants to make Him.

In a permissive, relativistic culture, the God of Christianity is often portrayed as a permissive God who affirms each individual's moral judgments. Or, in the case of those who are hateful toward any thought of God, He is slandered in ways that reveal a great ignorance of the scriptures. What ties both groups together is that they are people who *think* they know something about the Christian God.

What this means is that we cannot declare the gospel without a clear declaration of the true God. We must introduce people to the true God. Our starting place with sinners must not assume that because we might use the same vocabulary, we are operating with the same dictionary.

To take it a step further, the frightening reality is that this misinformation campaign has not just had an impact *outside* the professing church. In fact, wrong ideas about God are seated in our pews every Sunday morning. It is not just the world outside the church that needs to be introduced to the true God. It is to the professing church that we need to say, "here is your God—know Him!"

In the study of Nahum we come face to face with what I'm afraid is a strange God to many professing Christians. The God of Nahum is the God of the Bible, but is the God of Nahum your God? The God of Nahum is not just a God of love; He is a God of wrath. He is a jealous God, an avenging God, a thoroughly just God, and a God who never forgets when it comes to the matter of justice. He is a God who judges and disciplines His people by their enemies, and then judges their enemies in due time. This will become very clear as we make our way through the book.

In this chapter we will introduce the book of Nahum, and then beginning with the next chapter we will examine it systematically.

The book of Nahum is God's message of destruction and judgment upon the city of Nineveh. It is an oracle, a message of doom, against that city. At the same time, it serves as God's message of comfort to His people.

It is a book that is unique in so many ways:

It is unique in its form. It is described as a **book (סֵפֶר)**. A writing, a letter, a document, a book, is the meaning of the word. And there are internal indications that rather than this being the record of something that Nahum preached, it is simply a written record of the message that God gave him. For example, there are some who believe that in the first chapter there is a partial acrostic. If this is so, then it was written in a way to strike someone visually rather than audibly. And it *is* a poetic masterpiece. Nahum's writing is vivid and crisp and rapid in its movements. He makes use of multiple devices of communication to drive home the message that God gave him.

Kenneth Barker – "Longman and Dillard point out that the first verse calls Nahum's work a *sēper,* "book." This is significant since Nahum is the only one of the prophetic works thus named. Whereas most of the other prophets were at least initially preachers and their books were composed after their sermons, "Nahum, it appears, wrote a book." This suggestion is believed to be confirmed by the observation that some of Nahum's poetic devices, such as the partial acrostic in 1:2–8, are more visual than auditory."[1]

It is unique in its historical context. It is an oracle concerning Nineveh, the capital city of the Assyrian empire. This is the same Nineveh that was spared by God after it repented at the preaching of Jonah, just 100 years before. What this mean is that the book of Nahum is a testimony to the tragic wasting of God's mercies. God had mercy on Nineveh, then Nineveh threw that mercy away.

Nahum doesn't mention the reign of any kings, so it must be dated in a different way. We know that Nahum was written sometime between 663 and 612 BC, because it makes reference to the Assyrian conquest of Thebes, a city in Egypt that had been thought to be impregnable. That took place in 663. It predicts the destruction of Nineveh, which took place at the hands of the Babylonians and Medes in 612. But as you read the book, there are indications that Assyria is still at its high point in terms of strength. This would indicate that the book was written before the death of the Assyrian ruler named Ashurbanipal, and before 626 BC when the

---

[1] Kenneth L. Barker, *Micah, Nahum, Habakkuk, Zephaniah*, vol. 20, The New American Commentary (Nashville: Broadman & Holman Publishers, 1999), 147.

empire began to decline. Remember that Assyria conquered the northern kingdom (Israel) in 722. Judah had been in servitude to Assyria for some time as well, stretching back many years before that date. By the time that Nahum is written, the Assyrian empire had been the unquestioned world power for what seemed like forever, and it was a *cruel* master. Assyria was feared by everyone, and loved by no one. And God, through Nahum, announces Assyria's downfall at a time when it seems impossible.

This is written either when Manasseh was king in Judah (695-642), or during the early portion of Josiah's reign. It's possible that this message is given at a time when Josiah is leading the nation in repentant reforms, but it's more likely that it was written prior to that.

It is unique in its contrasts. Even the name of the prophet serves as an example of the kinds of contrasts found in the book. Nahum comes from a root that means comfort or compassion. This is the name of the man declaring a message that critics have called "a hymn of hate." The messenger's name is fitting, however, as God uses Nahum to comfort Judah.[2]

What is hateful to sinful man is beautiful in the sight of those who know the true God. The truth of God's faithful justice is a comfort to all who love righteousness. In fact, patience with men is found in the conviction that vengeance belongs to God.

It is unique in its theological emphases. It emphasizes that the true God is one who is glorious in the execution of wrath. It also emphasizes that nations exist by God's permission. When God decides that your time is over, there is nothing you can do to rescue yourself. That is a timeless lesson and an important lesson for our own nation. When any nation imagines itself to exist by anything other than the mercy and grace of God, it is in a dangerous state.

Nineveh was a magnificent city. It seemed unconquerable. There was an inner city, an outer city, and neighborhoods outside of that. The inner wall was 8 miles in circumference, and the outer wall longer than that. The inner wall was 100 feet high — wide enough for three chariots abreast — with a moat 60 feet deep and 150 feet wide.[3]

---

[2] Barker, 152.

[3] John MacArthur, *The MacArthur Bible Commentary* (Nashville: Thomas Nelson), 1022.

James Montgomery Boice – "Sennacherib's palace was called 'the Palace with No Rival.' It was of cedar, cypress, and alabaster. Lions of bronze and bulls of white marble guarded it. Its great hall measured forty by one hundred and fifty feet. Sennacherib's armory, where he kept his chariots, armor, horses, weapons, and other equipment, covered forty-six acres and took six years to build."[4]

It was the largest city in the world. It was the administrative hub of the Assyrian empire. And when Assyrian power was still at full strength, Yahweh says, through Nahum, that it's coming down.

So, as we think about the book as a whole, consider three personal lessons.

THE BOOK OF NAHUM TEACHES US THAT OUR CONCEPTION OF GOD IS OFTEN FAR TOO WEAK

The same God who is a God of love is also the God who executes wrath. It is God's glory to show mercy, but it is also God's glory to execute justice. The same God who offers gracious forgiveness is the God who declares that He is the one who will not clear the guilty.

Nahum 1:3 The LORD is slow to anger and great in power, and the LORD will by no means clear the guilty. His way is in whirlwind and storm, and the clouds are the dust of his feet.

When Nahum declares this truth about God, he is not declaring anything new. He is simply expositing what has been revealed about God in the Torah.

Exodus 34:6 The LORD passed before him and proclaimed, "The LORD, the LORD, a God merciful and gracious, slow to anger, and abounding in steadfast love and faithfulness, [7] keeping steadfast love for thousands, forgiving iniquity and transgression and sin, but who will by no means clear the guilty, visiting the iniquity of the fathers on the children and the children's children, to the third and the fourth generation (also: Num. 14:18).

---

[4] James Montgomery Boice, The Minor Prophets, vol.2 (Grand Rapids: Baker) 371-72.

James Montgomery Boice – "Many people do not like to think of God as a God of wrath. They prefer to think of Him as a God of sickly love and sentimental indulgence. What a weakening of the biblical concept of the only true God this is! It is true that God is a God of love and mercy — a holy love and an utterly undeserved and sovereign mercy. But it is also true that God is a God of wrath against sin. Peter describes him as being patient... not wanting anyone to perish (2 Peter 3:9), but even this welcome description is set in the context of God's sure, though postponed judgment: 'The day of the Lord will come like a thief. The heavens will disappear with a roar; the elements will be destroyed by fire, and the earth and everything in it will be laid bare' (v.10). This is the point at which Nahum begins his prophecy. Nahum means 'comfort,' but there is no comfort for Nineveh in what he speaks. For Nineveh, God is to be a God of vengeance. The city is to fall."[5]

Question: Are you ashamed of the wrath of God? I hear many reformed people rejoicing to talk about God in the terms of being beautiful, and sweet, and satisfying, and so they should! But I don't hear many people talking about God's wrath, and vengeance, and certain judgment upon sin and unredeemed sinners. The Bible is full of that message. If we are to declare the true God, we must tell the truth about His whole nature.

Question: Do you fully acknowledge God's hatred for sin when you think about your own life? Do you ever tremble at the thought of God's holiness? I think this neglect with respect to God's character is at the root of a lot of self-indulgent living in the church. People don't fear sin as they should, and they don't fear God as they should. People are often guilty of not thinking of liberty in terms of serving God and others, or the freedom to walk in holiness, but in terms of all the things they can do to indulge themselves. It is by the fear of the Lord that people depart from evil (Pro 3:7).

THE BOOK OF NAHUM TEACHES US THAT OUR CONCEPTION OF GOD IS OFTEN FAR TOO SMALL

As I read Nahum in its historical context, I am struck by how long the world must have seemed like a very dark place if you lived in Judah. Our nation is 241 years old as I write. Israel came into contact with the

---

[5] Boice, p.372.

expanding Assyrian empire in the middle 800's BC. Shalmaneser III (who reigned from 858-824 BC) received tribute from Jehu. The Jewish people, as Nahum is written, have been living in dread of this deadly and cruel enemy for around 200 years. Think about our nation and what it would be like to have a subservient relationship to a nation that was the moral and compassionate equivalent of ISIS, to have characterized our entire existence.

Tiglath-Pileser III (745-727 BC) invaded Judah and received tribute from Azariah. In 722 his son, Shalmaneser V, besieged Samaria. What he began, the next king, Sargon II finished. So, the northern kingdom had already fallen to Assyria many years before Nahum was written. In 701 BC Sennacherib invaded Judah and threatened Jerusalem. God miraculously spared Jerusalem during Hezekiah's reign (2 Kings 18-19).

This has been a long, long, time of terror. However, it has not been terror without a reason. The sins of God's people have exposed them to this terror. But now, God is bringing Nineveh to an end and Assyria to its knees. Even after Nahum's message, however, it is likely that the remnant of true believers had to wait another 30 years or so before it was executed.

We often have a short-term vision of our world because we have a self-centered view of God. What God does in our little brief lifetime is not even close to being the whole story. Our self-centered perspectives rob us of God-admiring and God-exalting praises, because we fail to recognize that God's eternality and sovereignty allow Him to be in no rush.

Question: How big is your conception of God? How do you understand Him to be working in history? Realize that this same kind of patient, sure, outworking of God's sovereign decrees, is at work in all the circumstances and events of your own life. God's work in your life is much bigger than the one thing that has your attention right now. His work in your life is much larger than the small snippets that you see and fear.

THE BOOK OF NAHUM TEACHES US THAT OUR CONCEPTION OF GOD IS OFTEN FAR TOO UNTRUSTING

Assyrian domination had been established for hundreds of years. When this prophecy is given, Assyria is still strong. The things Nahum pronounces would have seemed impossible. Assyrian military power had ruled the world. Assyrian threats, intimidation, and terror, had ruled the world. Assyrian religion had ruled the world. Where was Yahweh? Where was the God of the Bible? Where was the God of Israel?

Our God, the God of the Bible, the one true and living God, the God and Father of our Lord Jesus Christ, IS. He is not absent. He is a rewarder of those who diligently seek Him. He does not forget, and He ordains symmetry in many of His dealings with His world.

His providence and wisdom are on display. Assyria conquering Thebes indicates that the impregnable is not impregnable at all! What we conquer only points to the reality that *we can be conquered*, and when God determines destruction, no one can stay His hand.

Nahum 3:8 Are you better than Thebes that sat by the Nile, with water around her, her rampart a sea, and water her wall? 9 Cush was her strength; Egypt too, and that without limit; Put and the Libyans were her helpers. 10 Yet she became an exile; she went into captivity; her infants were dashed in pieces at the head of every street; for her honored men lots were cast, and all her great men were bound in chains. 11 You also will be drunken; you will go into hiding; you will seek a refuge from the enemy. 12 All your fortresses are like fig trees with first-ripe figs—if shaken they fall into the mouth of the eater. 13 Behold, your troops are women in your midst. The gates of your land are wide open to your enemies; fire has devoured your bars. 14 Draw water for the siege; strengthen your forts; go into the clay; tread the mortar; take hold of the brick mold! 15 There will the fire devour you; the sword will cut you off. It will devour you like the locust. Multiply yourselves like the locust; multiply like the grasshopper!

What this means is that no matter what the world looks like at the moment, we know that God is and that He is a rewarder of those who diligently seek Him (Heb 11:6).

Revelation 21:1 Then I saw a new heaven and a new earth, for the first heaven and the first earth had passed away, and the sea was no more. 2 And I saw the holy city, new Jerusalem, coming down out of heaven from God, prepared as a bride adorned for her husband. 3 And I heard a loud voice from the throne saying, "Behold, the dwelling place of God is with man. He will dwell with them, and they will be his people, and God himself will be with them as their God. 4 He will wipe away every tear from their eyes, and death shall be no more, neither shall there be mourning, nor crying, nor pain anymore, for the former things have passed away." 5 And he who was seated on the throne said, "Behold, I am making all things new." Also he said, "Write this down, for these words are trustworthy and true." 6 And he said to me, "It is done! I am the Alpha and the Omega, the beginning and the end. To the thirsty I will give from the spring of the water of life without payment. [7] The one who conquers will have this heritage, and I will be his God and he will be my son. [8] But as for the cowardly, the faithless, the detestable, as for murderers, the sexually immoral, sorcerers, idolaters, and all liars, their portion will be in the lake that burns with fire and sulfur, which is the second death."

2
THE GOD WHO DETERMINES ALL THINGS
(1:1-8)

God is at the center of every picture that is being viewed rightly. He is the determiner of everything. Every individual, every situation, turns one way or another, experiences one outcome or another, depending upon how that person or how that situation is related to the true God.

There are precious lives sitting before me every Sunday morning. There are futures, destinies, represented in every worship setting. There are decisions that are being made, and that will be made in the days to come, represented in the congregation. And all of those lives, all of those destinies, the outcome of all of those decisions, hinge on what their relationship to God is and will be.

That is what we see in this section of Nahum. In this first chapter we see a burdened prophet, we see a foolish nation, we see a comforted people, and standing at the center of the picture is an awesome God—the only true and living God. And this God, the true and living God, is making Himself known through a prophet named Nahum. God is declaring Himself. He is declaring His nature and character. He is declaring His abilities. He is declaring His commitments. And, as a result of who He is, and what He does, and what He will not do, He is declaring the current condition and the future destinies of all the others in this scene.

As I already noted, the same is true for every individual and every situation that exists in this world. Who you are as a person, what your current condition is, what your future is going to be, the way you're going to live, and the choices you're going to make, are all determined by what your relationship is, and will be, to the God of the Bible.

When Nahum records this prophecy, it is sometime between 663 and 626 BC. It is either during the reign of Manasseh or Josiah in Judah. The cruel and fierce Assyrian empire rules the world. They have already conquered Samaria and the northern kingdom in 722 BC. They invaded Judah in 701 BC, and when they tried to take Jerusalem they suffered the massive loss of 185,000 men due to God miraculously saving the city (2 Kings 19:35). But the Assyrians have recovered from that. They are still strong, and they are still feared by all the peoples of the world, when God tells them what their future will be.

THE BURDENED PROPHET (vs.1)

God gives this word through a prophet named Nahum. What He gave to Nahum represented a burden. The word that is translated "oracle" comes from a verb that means "to be lifted or to be carried." It is a weighty message that Nahum carries on behalf of God. It is a great responsibility to communicate the Word of God.

That hasn't changed. No one should take God's Word into their mouth unless they are mindful of the weightiness of the message they declare. The weightiness of the message must be felt in terms of the responsibility of the one who communicates the message, and in terms of the ones being addressed.

God is at the center of that picture. The message is weighty because it is God's message. A true God, a living God, an almighty God, a sovereign God, is the one who is the ultimate author of the message that Nahum delivers.

We know nothing about the man who communicated the message. We know that his name comes from a Hebrew root that means "comfort." Beyond that, we know nothing except that he was an Elkoshite. That is, he came from a place called Elkosh. No one today knows for certain where that place was located. It is most likely that it was a place in the north of the land of Israel, but by the time that Nahum writes he is living in Judah, perhaps in Jerusalem.

What Nahum gives us here is called: An oracle (burden), a book, a vision. That threefold description makes clear that he is not communicating his own message. The words oracle and vision make clear what the nature of the book really is. Nahum is simply the messenger (in this book) of God's Word concerning Nineveh, the capital city of the Assyrian empire.

And, after that very brief self-description, Nahum immediately turns his attention to the declaration of the God who gives this message. So, the very way that Nahum constructs this makes plain that God is to be at the center of the picture.

Which brings us to the second movement within this chapter.

THE AWESOME GOD (vs.2-8)

Immediately, God puts His own character and nature on display. He tells us who He is, what He does, what He will not do, and what the results are. The picture that emerges is that of an awe-inspiring God.

Who He Is: The True God Is a God of Vengeance (vs.2)

Three times in verse 2, God tells us about His vengeance. To say that God is a God of vengeance, or an avenging God, is to say that He is the God who repays. He repays in defense of His own name and glory. He repays in defense of His people. He is a God who punishes what is wrong, what is unjust. He is a God of justice. He is a God who knows, who remembers, and dispenses justice.

Who He Is: The True God Is a God of Jealousy (vs.2)

God is a jealous God, which means He is a God who is zealous on behalf of His own reputation, of His own will, and of His own people. It might be helpful to think of this as zeal for one's own property, for what rightfully belongs to oneself.

God's vengeance is tied to His jealousy. His vengeance is Him repaying His enemies as a result of His zeal for His own rightful honor. He repays the enemies of His people as a result of His zeal for His children. He repays those who have rebelled against His will as a result of His zeal for righteousness.

You will see that emphasis in verse 2. It is against the adversaries of God, the enemies of God, that this avenging activity is vented. And yet, as you read the entire account, it becomes plain that God is also defending His people. *When one sets himself in opposition to the people of God, he has made himself God's enemy in a special way.*

1 Corinthians 3:16 Do you not know that you are God's temple and that God's Spirit dwells in you? 17 If anyone destroys God's temple, God will destroy him. For God's temple is holy, and you are that temple.

Who He Is: The True God Is Wrathful (vs.2)

The vengeance of God is no mild thing. He defends and repays with a hot rage. He is a God who knows of sin and executes wrath against sin. He is a God who hates that which does not represent His glory. He hates sin and evil in all its forms. There is a holy anger in God toward everything that is in opposition to His holy character.

This knowledge of God's character is something that His people have made use of in their pleadings.

Psalm 7:1 *A Shiggaion of David, which he sang to the LORD concerning the words of Cush, a Benjaminite.* O LORD my God, in you do I take refuge; save me from all my pursuers and deliver me, 2 lest like a lion they tear my soul apart, rending it in pieces, with none to deliver. 3 O LORD my God, if I have done this, if there is wrong in my hands, 4 if I have repaid my friend with evil or plundered my enemy without cause, 5 let the enemy pursue my soul and overtake it, and let him trample my life to the ground and lay my glory in the dust. Selah 6 Arise, O LORD, in your anger; lift yourself up against the fury of my enemies; awake for me; you have appointed a judgment. 7 Let the assembly of the peoples be gathered about you; over it return on high. 8 The LORD judges the peoples; judge me, O LORD, according to my righteousness and according to the integrity that is in me. 9 Oh, let the evil of the wicked come to an end, and may you establish the righteous-- you who test the minds and hearts, O righteous God! 10 My shield is with God, who saves the upright in heart. 11 God is a righteous judge, and a God who feels indignation every day. 12 If a man does not repent, God will whet his sword; he has bent and readied his bow; 13 he has prepared for him his deadly weapons, making his arrows fiery shafts. 14 Behold, the wicked man conceives evil and is pregnant with mischief and gives birth to lies. 15 He makes a pit, digging it out, and falls into the hole that he has made. 16 His mischief returns upon his own head, and on his own skull his violence descends. 17 I will give to the LORD the thanks due to his righteousness, and I will sing praise to the name of the LORD, the Most High.

Who He Is: The True God Is Slow to Anger (vs.3)

He is a God who knows and demonstrates a hot anger toward sin and rebels, but He is not capricious. He is not a God of sudden outbursts of anger. That is not to say that God never moves swiftly against sin. But, it is to say that it is His character and nature to be patient and merciful, and all that He does in His anger towards sin reflects His perfect wisdom and a perfectly measured response. It is God's nature to desire mercy instead of judgment.

Who He Is: The True God Is Great in Power (vs.3-6)

His patience does not diminish His strength. His patience must never be confused with weakness or forgetfulness or any kind of compromise with evil.

God's judgment is comparable to a great dam filling with water, so much water that when it is released it will destroy everything it comes in contact with. God is the one controlling the dam, so that the only thing sparing the enemies of God at this very moment is the God against whom they rage. When the time comes—when God is sovereignly finished with His own patience, and opens the door of the dam of His wrath, His power will be evident. His strength will be overwhelming, because it is infinite.

In fact, He illustrates this through Nahum:

The power of God is seen in the whirlwind–the tornado.
The power of God is seen in the great storm.
The power of God is realized in the massiveness of creation.
The power of God is demonstrated by His control over creation.

It is God who can dry up the sea (vs.4). It is God who can cause places that are normally fertile and rich to become barren places (vs.4). It is God who can shake the earth and its inhabitants (vs.5). And, isn't it instructive that Nahum doesn't attribute these things to nature but to God? Or, to put it more accurately, God does not allow us to attribute these things to nature. He attributes these things to Himself.

Question: Can you see that when the world is full of rebellion against God and then sees drought, frozen conditions, diseases, heat waves, flooding, earthquakes, and then doesn't blame its sins against God, but its sins *against the planet,* how it calls for the wrath of God? Man doesn't control the planet. The planet doesn't control itself. God controls the planet. Everything He has made is subject to Him.

Who He Is: The True God Is Good and Knows His Own (vs.7)

God's judgments are never mistaken. He knows His friends from His enemies. He knows His children from all pretenders. He knows those who stand forgiven because they have looked to His mercy in His Son, and those who are still in their sins no matter how religious they may be.

His judgments are always on the side of what is right. His judgments always reflect absolute holiness and purity. His anger is a just anger. His punishments are just punishments. He is a place of safety (stronghold) for all those who trust in Him. His people are those who take refuge in Him, and He proves Himself a faithful protector in the day of trouble and distress. This is the true God: A God of vengeance, holy jealousy, and wrath. A God who is slow to anger, great in power, and is good—a stronghold to those who take refuge in Him. This is who God is.

What does He do?

What God Does: He Takes Vengeance and Reserves Wrath (vs.2)

God can be trusted to act in accordance with His holy nature. It is not enough to know that God is a jealous and avenging God. We must also be convinced that unless we meet with Him on the ground of true repentance, looking to Him for the mercy that is found in His provision for our sins (His Son's death on the cross), we will fall into the hands of that vengeful and justly angry God. God actually takes vengeance on His adversaries and He does not forget their deeds that deserve His wrath.

What God Does: He Puts His Power on Display by His Dealings With Nature (vs.4-5)

This reminds us that God has not stepped away from what He created. It does not run on its own. It is all subject to Him and obeys His voice.

What God Does: He Protects His People and Punishes His Enemies (vs.7-8)

Nahum 1:7 The LORD is good, a stronghold in the day of trouble; he knows those who take refuge in him. [8] But with an overflowing flood he will make a complete end of the adversaries, and will pursue his enemies into darkness.

3
WRATH OR REFUGE?
(1:9-15)

God has told us who He is, what He does, what He will not do, and—in general terms—what that means in terms of an outcome.

We were reminded in the previous section that God is:
- A God of vengeance, jealousy, wrath
- One who is slow to anger
- One who is great in power
- One who is good and knows His own.

We were reminded that because of who He is:
- He takes vengeance and reserves wrath.
- He puts His power on display.
- He protects His people and punishes their enemies.
- He will not clear the guilty.

The result is that the person who is God's enemy cannot stand, cannot endure, cannot survive, and will not escape. If we take refuge in God, we are safe.

But these truths are never to be considered in strictly generic terms. What God reveals has *personal application.* What God reveals finds meaning in the real world and in the current situation. These are not truths with applications restricted to a time long ago. These truths mean something for your own life and the lives of those around you. What God has revealed has application to groups of people—to nations. It has meaning for the current world scene.

This is what our God does in verses 9-15. He takes what He has declared in general terms, and He makes specific application. Having told us who He is, He now declares the implications of who He is for the Assyrian people and for His own people. He does this in an alternating fashion. God is who He is; how they relate to Him determines their present state and their future expectations.

THE FUTILITY OF ASSYRIAN PLANS (vs.9-11)

Sennacherib tried to take Jerusalem in 701 BC. He and his forces were turned back as God acted in a miraculous way to deliver the city. He lost 185,000 men in the process (2 Ki 18-19). He later met with his end.

2 Kings 19:35 And that night the angel of the LORD went out and struck down 185,000 in the camp of the Assyrians. And when people arose early in the morning, behold, these were all dead bodies. [36] Then Sennacherib king of Assyria departed and went home and lived at Nineveh. [37] And as he was worshiping in the house of Nisroch his god, Adrammelech and Sharezer, his sons, struck him down with the sword and escaped into the land of Ararat. And Esarhaddon his son reigned in his place.

But, following that, the Assyrians continued to expand and be strengthened, and Nineveh was expanded and beautified. Apparently, the Assyrians continued to strategize about how to take the city of Jerusalem.

God speaks directly to the Assyrian plans and tells them that they plot in vain. In addition, He tells them three things about such plans. He tells them that their plans will not come to pass (vs.9). He tells them that their future will be characterized by confusion and consumption (vs.10). And He tells them that their counsels are corrupt (vs.11).

We are not sure who God has in mind in verse 11, but it doesn't matter. Whether it looks back on Sennacherib as an example of their worthless counselors, or to someone who has emerged since, God is telling them in advance that what they are thinking about is absolutely futile. Sennacherib was a model of this futility.

2 Kings 19:10 "Thus shall you speak to Hezekiah king of Judah: 'Do not let your God in whom you trust deceive you by promising that Jerusalem will not be given into the hand of the king of Assyria. [11] Behold, you have heard what the kings of Assyria have done to all lands, devoting them to destruction. And shall you be delivered? [12] Have the gods of the nations delivered them, the nations that my fathers destroyed, Gozan, Haran, Rezeph, and the people of Eden who were in Telassar? [13] Where is the king of Hamath, the king of Arpad, the king of the city of Sepharvaim, the king of Hena, or the king of Ivvah?"

From every human point of view, these threats represented the truth. The history of resistance had proven vain. But what the Assyrians did not know and did not believe was that it was actually Israel's God who had allowed their successes for a time, and would now tear them to the ground.

Note: It is interesting that there is the mention of drunkenness, because drunkenness played a role in the eventual destruction of Nineveh and we will learn more about that when we get into Nahum chapter two.

Question: What do you think becomes of your plans that do not reflect submission to God and His will?

THE END OF JUDAH'S OPPRESSION (vs.12-13)

God not only speaks direct words of judgment; He also speaks direct words of comfort. Oh, the joy of hearing comfort from God! What peace there is when you know that the living God is your defender and refuge!

God acknowledges the very real strength of Assyria, but promises their destruction (vs.12).

God acknowledges the very real presence of His discipline, but promises its end (vs.12b).

God acknowledges the very real yoke of Assyria's oppression, but promises deliverance (vs.13).

To trust in the God of the Bible is not to deny reality. It is to acknowledge His sovereignty over all realities. We are not a people who have to stick our heads in the sand to be able to cope; we are a people who lift up our eyes and look to the one who is in control of all things, and we find our rest in Him. This, of course, requires that we are really one of His people, and that we are trusting in Him.

THE DEATH SENTENCE FOR ASSYRIA (vs.14)

The Lord now turns His attention back to Nineveh, and by extension, the Assyrians. God has issued a command. What God commands (in the sense of a decree), all of creation obeys. The Lord has given commandment about the city.

It will meet with an absolute end (vs.14a)

Indeed, Nineveh did meet with an absolute and devastating end. It is possible that this verse is addressed to the Assyrian king. But, given the context, I think it is better to take this as a word concerning the city itself, addressed in a personified manner.

Kenneth Barker – "Part one involved the future of the people of Nineveh. One of the most sorrowful tragedies of ancient peoples involved not producing offspring who would carry on the family name (see Deut 7:24; 29:20; 1 Sam 24:21). Even contemporary people feel the sorrow of the end of the family name. God commanded that the Assyrian destruction would be of such magnitude that the nation would have no offspring (lit., "seed") to carry on its name. The memory of one's name was very important to Near Eastern royalty. "Ashurbanipal (669–627 b.c.), the last great king of Assyria, prays that the son who follows him would honor and preserve his name on the building inscriptions he had carved as his own memorial. But the decree of God declares that no one shall survive to maintain his name."[6]

Elliott Johnson – "Nineveh was never rebuilt. So complete was its destruction that when Xenophon passed by the site about 200 years later, he thought the mounds were the ruins of some other city. And Alexander the Great, fighting in a battle nearby, did not realize that he was near the ruins of Nineveh."[7]

---

[6] Kenneth L. Barker, *Micah, Nahum, Habakkuk, Zephaniah*, vol. 20, The New American Commentary (Nashville: Broadman & Holman Publishers, 1999), 188.

[7] Elliott E. Johnson, "Nahum," in *The Bible Knowledge Commentary: An Exposition of the Scriptures*, ed. J. F. Walvoord and R. B. Zuck, vol. 1 (Wheaton, IL: Victor Books, 1985), 1499.

Its power and religion will be destroyed (vs.14b)

The Assyrians boasted in their false gods. The true God would expose them.

Note: People still speak boastful words. In fact, it has become fashionable. It is the new morality, it is the new righteousness, to "believe in yourself." People profess their own strength, their own rights, their own priority, and sadly, it will all be exposed as empty in due time.

Its grave will be determined by God (vs.14c)

The word for "vile" has the meaning of small or light. It means to be of little account. Assyria suffers from a sense of self-importance. God tells them of their true moral weight, and they are found wanting. They are light, they are small, and God will bury them; He will put them in the grave.

Revelation 20:12 And I saw the dead, great and small, standing before the throne, and books were opened. Then another book was opened, which is the book of life. And the dead were judged by what was written in the books, according to what they had done. [13] And the sea gave up the dead who were in it, Death and Hades gave up the dead who were in them, and they were judged, each one of them, according to what they had done. [14] Then Death and Hades were thrown into the lake of fire. This is the second death, the lake of fire. [15] And if anyone's name was not found written in the book of life, he was thrown into the lake of fire.

THE CALL FOR JUDAH'S WORSHIP (vs.15)

God's judgment upon the wicked means God's deliverance for His people. Though they would have to wait for this to be done in time and history, God announces it as though it is already done. The messengers are pictured as standing on the mountains all around the city of Jerusalem and announcing the news.

When Assyria is broken, the people of God will once again be able to celebrate their feasts and carry out their worship. Assyria will never trouble them again.

Question: How do these truths about our sovereign God change your world view?

Are you in the place of having taken refuge in Him? Are you His enemy? Perhaps you are His wayward child standing in the place of discipline. Will your turn from your sins and take refuge in Him? When we have taken refuge in Him, and heard His words of comfort, doesn't that call for our joyful worship and praise? Do you realize that outside of God's Son, the Lord Jesus Christ, there is no refuge for the sinner?

Romans 10:13 For "everyone who calls on the name of the Lord will be saved." 14 How then will they call on him in whom they have not believed? And how are they to believe in him of whom they have never heard? And how are they to hear without someone preaching? 15 And how are they to preach unless they are sent? As it is written, "How beautiful are the feet of those who preach the good news!"

4
DESTRUCTION DECLARED
(2:1-13)

It is God's unique glory to be able to announce the end from the beginning. If the God of the Bible really exists, then He is eternal, all-knowing, all-powerful and sovereign. That means He can tell us what He has determined to do before He does it. He can tell us what will come to pass, because He is the one who brings it into being. As the Biblical record makes plain, the God of the Bible does exist, and He has proven Himself able to tell the story of the future.

The gods of men, the false gods that represent demonic activity and fleshly imagination—that serve as the face for demonic and fleshly deception—cannot do this. They do not create, they do not support, and they do not communicate, because they do not exist! Whatever *is communicated* in the names of those false gods, is a lie. The true God is the creator, the sustainer, and the determiner of all things. He is absolutely truthful and perfectly accurate in everything that He reveals. He is able to speak and to act because He really exists.

The God of the Bible made this plain through His prophet Isaiah:

Isaiah 46:1 Bel bows down; Nebo stoops; their idols are on beasts and livestock; these things you carry are borne as burdens on weary beasts. [2] They stoop; they bow down together; they cannot save the burden, but themselves go into captivity. [3] "Listen to me, O house of Jacob, all the remnant of the house of Israel, who have been borne by me from before your birth, carried from the womb; [4] even to your old age I am he, and to gray hairs I will carry you. I have made, and I will bear; I will carry and will save. [5] "To whom will you liken me and make me equal, and compare me, that we may be alike? [6] Those who lavish gold from the purse, and weigh out silver in the scales, hire a goldsmith, and he makes it into a god; then they fall down and worship! ⁷ They lift it to their shoulders, they carry it, they set it in its place, and it stands there; it cannot move from its place. If one cries to it, it does not answer or save him from his trouble. ⁸ "Remember this and stand firm, recall it to mind, you transgressors, ⁹ remember the former things of old; for I am God, and there is no other; I am God, and there is none like me, ¹⁰ declaring the end from the beginning and from ancient times things not yet done, saying, 'My counsel shall stand, and I will accomplish all my purpose,' ¹¹ calling a bird of prey from the east, the man of my counsel from a far country. I have spoken, and I will bring it to pass; I have purposed, and I will do it.

It is that God who now speaks through the prophet Nahum. And in this second chapter, He is declaring disaster. He is declaring destruction. He said in the first chapter that He will destroy Nineveh, that the Assyrian empire is headed for a great fall. Now, in chapter two, God describes it in vivid terms—but not after the fact. He describes it in advance of its happening. The destruction has not yet arrived, but the God of the Bible is able to describe it with vivid and perfect accuracy, as history went on to confirm. He is able to do this because He is the one who will destroy them. He is not held captive by the future. He determines the future.

Note: That truth speaks soberly to our generation. It communicates a sober message to everyone who hears Nahum's message, and everyone to whom they, in turn, communicate it. What God does here with respect to Nineveh, He has also done with respect to the future of the world. He has done this with respect to all lost humanity and their final judgment. If God was proven truthful when He said He would destroy Nineveh, then He is to be feared when He says that the entire world outside of Christ is headed for a final judgment that ends in hell. The same God who said He would destroy Nineveh—and did—has already described what the scene will be like before the Great White Throne Judgment.

Revelation 20:11 Then I saw a great white throne and him who was seated on it. From his presence earth and sky fled away, and no place was found for them. ¹² And I saw the dead, great and small, standing before the throne, and books were opened. Then another book was opened, which is the book of life. And the dead were judged by what was written in the books, according to what they had done. ¹³ And the sea gave up the dead who were in it, Death and Hades gave up the dead who were in them, and they were judged, each one of them, according to what they had done. ¹⁴ Then Death and Hades were thrown into the lake of fire. This is the second death, the lake of fire. ¹⁵ And if anyone's name was not found written in the book of life, he was thrown into the lake of fire.

If Assyria should have feared God, then every human being should fear God. In this chapter we see the glory of the living God. He declares destruction before it arrives.

THE SOUND OF DESTRUCTION (vs.1-2)

God is speaking to the city of Nineveh. He is also speaking, by extension, to the Assyrian empire. What He is declaring is the application of His nature and character—attributes that were described in the first chapter. He is a God of vengeance...of holy jealousy...of wrath. His commitment to justice is unswerving. He will by no means clear the guilty. He is slow to anger, but great in power. Just because His judgment has not yet arrived doesn't mean that it won't arrive. He is good. His judgments are absolutely right in every way. He is a stronghold for His people, so that He defends them. This means that when you mistreat His people, you are His enemy and He will repay. When you mistreat anyone, divine justice returns it on your head.

What God's nature and character means for Assyria is that what she has dealt out to others in the past, and what she plots against God by plotting against His people, she will experience herself. God's vengeance will be felt as a result of a scattering force that He will send against her.

God issues a call. He sounds the trumpet. He does this in a vivid way as though the conquering forces are already at the walls of this great city. He envisions that scattering force (which we know from history was made up of the Medes and Scythians) at the walls of Nineveh, and calls upon the city to prepare for what she is about to experience.

The Call from God: Man the Ramparts (vs.1) The ramparts refer to the tops of the fortified walls.

The Call from God: Watch the Road (vs.1) That is, keep on the lookout for the invading forces.

The Call from God: Dress for Battle (vs.1) That is, gird up your loins.

The Call from God: Gather Your Strength (vs.1)
This is very interesting. God is saying, "get ready." He doesn't have to surprise them. He can call them to readiness and still defeat them. He can call them to readiness and WILL defeat them!

The Green Bay Packers football team of the 1960's won championships five times in seven years. They did not win because they fooled people. Everyone knew what was coming. The Packers were famous for the power sweep. "A seal block here, a seal block here, and the back runs in the alley!" In effect, they announced "We are coming, stop us if you can." And, in those championship years, no one could.

God is all-powerful. He is all-wise. He is always-present. He is sovereign—not only over nature and circumstances, but over the hearts and minds of people. He cannot be defeated. No preparation, no defense, can stand against Him.

The Cause of God (vs.2)

The Lord declares the cause for which He is doing this. He is carrying out His vengeance, His jealousy, His wrath. He is restoring the honor and power ("majesty" means to lift up, height, eminence, exaltation) of His people. And by saying, "as the majesty of Israel" the Lord may be saying that just as He has already promised to restore the honor and power of the northern kingdom in the future, so He now promises to restore the majesty of Judah as well.

Hosea 14:1 Return, O Israel, to the LORD your God, for you have stumbled because of your iniquity. ² Take with you words and return to the LORD; say to him, "Take away all iniquity; accept what is good, and we will pay with bulls the vows of our lips. ³ Assyria shall not save us; we will not ride on horses; and we will say no more, 'Our God,' to the work of our hands. In you the orphan finds mercy." ⁴ I will heal their apostasy; I will love them freely, for my anger has turned from them. ⁵ I will be like the dew to Israel; he shall blossom like the lily; he shall take root like the trees of Lebanon; ⁶ his shoots shall spread out; his beauty shall be like the olive, and his fragrance like Lebanon. ⁷ They shall return and dwell beneath my shadow; they shall flourish like the grain; they shall blossom like the vine; their fame shall be like the wine of Lebanon.

Or, Jacob and Israel may be used interchangeably in this context to refer to the people of God as a whole.

Carl Armerding – "Both usages are applied to Jacob, the latter being clearly intended here. In the poetic parallelism, "Jacob" and "Israel" represent the same entity (Ge 32:28; cf. 1 Ch 16:17; Ps 105:23; Hos 12:12), denoting the full twelve tribes descended from Jacob."[8]

Regardless, what is plain is that God has declared destruction for Assyria and exaltation for His people. What is also plain is the symmetry in the justice that is being meted out through this. God's people have been devastated, plundered, and their branches (pictured as a vine) have been ruined. So, now Assyria will be plundered.

THE SCENE OF DESTRUCTION (vs.3-10)

What we have next is one of the most vivid depictions of ancient warfare found anywhere in the Bible. The antecedent of the word "his" in 2:3 is the "scatterer" of verse 1, not the city of Nineveh. This is a description of the conquering forces coming upon the city of Nineveh as it is about to be destroyed.

The Appearance of the Enemy Forces (vs.3)

The Red Shields (vs.3a)
The Scarlet Uniforms (vs.3b)
The Flashing Chariots (vs.3c)
The Brandished Spears (vs.3d)

The Hebrew word translated "brandished" means "to shake." God gives a vivid mental image of the forces that will conquer the city, down to the shaking of their spears!

The Activity of the Enemy Forces (vs.4-5)

The Racing Chariots (vs.4): We see their speed. We see their course (the streets and squares outside the inner wall). We see their appearance (the light flashing off the polished metal).

The Advancing Soldiers (vs.5): Orders are given. Difficulty is ignored as the soldiers continue forward though they stumble. The wall is achieved. The siege device is set in place.

The Success of the Enemy Forces (vs.6-10)

---

[8] Carl E. Armerding, "Nahum," in *The Expositor's Bible Commentary: Daniel–Malachi (Revised Edition)*, ed. Tremper Longman III and David E. Garland, vol. 8 (Grand Rapids, MI: Zondervan, 2008), 580.

The Wall is Flooded (vs.6): This is an amazing scene.

Armerding – "This brief verse (five Hebrew words) marks a decisive turning point in the campaign, as the main line of defense is broken and the heart of the city destroyed. The noun 'river' is plural in Hebrew, and in fact Nineveh lay at the confluence of three rivers. The Tigris flowed close to its walls, and two tributaries, the Khosr and the Tebiltu, passed through the city itself. Virtually all of Nineveh's fifteen gates gave access also to one of these rivers or to a canal derived from them, thus being designated "gates of the rivers." Alternatively, the "gates" are those controlling the flow of the rivers rather than those giving access to the city. All three rivers were capable of rising to flood proportions when swollen by rain, and the inscriptions of Sennacherib repeatedly describe both the undermining effects of flood on the walls and buildings and the extensive damage or sluicing operations required to correct the problems.

It is possible, therefore, that the 'river gates' envisaged are those regulating the flow of water through one or more of these dams; indeed, the Akkadian term "gate of the river" (*bab-nari*) was applied to a canal gate by Sennacherib. When "thrown open" by the enemy, who already controlled the suburbs where they were situated, the gates would release a deluge of water, as a result of which the palace "collapses." The Assyrians flooded other cities themselves; it is fitting that their own city, corrupt and full of violence, should perish in the same manner. The verb *mûg* means "to melt" ("collapses," NIV). Its literal usage is primarily of dissolution by water, providing further corroboration for the preceding interpretation."[9]

The City is Humiliated (vs.7): "Its mistress is stripped" could possibly refer to the false goddess Ishtar being taken away into exile. Others have suggested that the queen was stripped naked and taken out of the city. If this refers to the false goddess, then the temple prostitutes (slave girls) are the ones lamenting and moaning on their way out of the city.

The Inhabitants Are Fleeing (vs.8): The meaning of the Hebrew is uncertain, but the NASB translates this: "Though Nineveh was like a pool of water throughout her days, Now they are fleeing." Nahum pictures the attempt to stop the retreat, but it goes unheeded.

The Wealth Is Plundered (vs.9): The description of plunder that cannot be accounted is no exaggeration. This is the capital city of an empire that has

---

[9] Armerding, 584–585.

been carrying off riches from other cities and other nations for hundreds of years. There is no way to envision all that would have been carried off when the city was destroyed.

The Ruin Is Felt (vs.10): There is a sickness that has set in when the people who oppressed others, intimidated others, acted cruelly toward others, now find themselves at the mercy of conquering foes.

THE SOBRIETY OF DESTRUCTION (vs.11-12)

What happened to the lion? What happened to mighty Assyria? The truth is put forth in a mocking way. It is a rhetorical question that demonstrates through the metaphor being employed what the point is. Assyria has been like a lion that terrorized everyone else. Assyria had killed and tortured, done so with delight, and until its ruthless heart was satisfied. But where is the lion now? What has become of it! The previous verses have told the story, and the pronouncement that follows will make it certain.

Ralph L. Smith – "This section is a taunt song addressed to Nineveh. It could have been used in a cultic celebration. The language shifts from that of a battle account to a metaphor of a lion's den. The passage opens with two rhetorical questions asking where the lions' dens are, now that Nineveh has been destroyed. It recalls how Assyria as a lion had plundered other peoples, strangling, tearing flesh, and carrying off prey to her cubs in their safe places in Nineveh. But now the tables have been turned. Behold, Yahweh is against Nineveh. That sealed her fate (cf. 3:5). Her military power will certainly be broken. Her soldiers will die by the sword, and her messengers (tax collectors) will no longer threaten other people."[10]

THE SURENESS OF DESTRUCTION (vs.13)

All of this is an absolute certainty.

Romans 8:31 What then shall we say to these things? If God is for us, who can be against us?

What a sweet promise Romans 8:31 is to the heart of a believer! But turn that promise around! If God is against you, who can help you?

---

[10] Ralph L. Smith, *Micah–Malachi*, vol. 32, Word Biblical Commentary (Dallas: Word, Incorporated, 1998), 84.

The Lord Is Against Nineveh
The Lord Will Turn the Tables on Nineveh
The Lord Will End Their Hunting
The Lord Will Silence Their Voices

And it all came to pass! This is God's unique glory. He tells the end before it arrives.

Question: So what will be your end?

Take note of the contrast between two "forevers" declared by God in His Word.

Revelation 19:1 After this I heard what seemed to be the loud voice of a great multitude in heaven, crying out, "Hallelujah! Salvation and glory and power belong to our God, 2 for his judgments are true and just; for he has judged the great prostitute who corrupted the earth with her immorality, and has avenged on her the blood of his servants." 3 Once more they cried out, "Hallelujah! The smoke from her goes up forever and ever."

Revelation 22:1 Then the angel showed me the river of the water of life, bright as crystal, flowing from the throne of God and of the Lamb 2 through the middle of the street of the city; also, on either side of the river, the tree of life with its twelve kinds of fruit, yielding its fruit each month. The leaves of the tree were for the healing of the nations. 3 No longer will there be anything accursed, but the throne of God and of the Lamb will be in it, and his servants will worship him. 4 They will see his face, and his name will be on their foreheads. 5 And night will be no more. They will need no light of lamp or sun, for the Lord God will be their light, and they will reign forever and ever.

We see a future of destruction and a future of delight. God declares both to be a certainty. To which do you belong?

5
CRIMES AND PUNISHMENT
(3:1-19)

The message of Nahum is a simple one. Anyone looking for some deep spiritual message hiding below the surface of the prophecy will be disappointed. Its message is straightforward, and powerfully so. It is meant to be heeded in a straightforward manner.

To the rebellious sinner it speaks of God's faithfulness to His own righteousness and to His people. The truth calls for repentance.

To the child of God that same commitment calls for our hope, and our peace, and our joy. When it seems that evil triumphs, you can be sure that it only SEEMS that way.

When you are strong, in worldly terms, without God, it is only for a season. When you seem strong without God, the time will come when your true weakness will be exposed. When you seem to prosper for a season as you mock the true God, and when you celebrate your false gods, and when you declare your superiority over those who trust the true God, you had better understand that the day is soon coming when your strength will be turned to weakness. Your rejoicing will be turned to grief. Imagined independence from the God of the Bible always leads to the grave.

And for those ***who trust in the true God***, though you may sorrow in the present, and experience pain in the present, you can rejoice in your future. The true God is sovereign, and His name will be vindicated. You can run into the strong tower of the name of God and know that you are ultimately safe.

Nineveh had been spared once. God sent a prophet to declare her doom, and she actually listened. God had mercy on her. Then she forgot that mercy. She ultimately continued in her blood-thirsty ways. Future generations rejected that mercy. God—now through Nahum—does not declare mercy to her. He declares doom, and He declares doom in the hearing of His people.

Though God speaks to Nineveh in this prophecy, the audience is Judah. God is speaking to Nineveh in the hearing of His people. Why? He does this because He wants His people to know that His judgment upon sin, the vindication of His own honor, and the defense of His own people, is not delayed forever.

Justice is coming, and though they have to wait a little while, they can be sure that it will arrive. That is what we see in this chapter. We see God detailing some of the many crimes of Nineveh, of the Assyrian empire, and we see God declaring destruction as a result. The final chapter can be organized into three parts. We see the bloody city ruined but without comfort (vs.1-7), the proud city hiding but without safety (vs.8-11), and the helpless city wounded but without sympathy (vs.12-19).

The message running through it all is that if you are God's enemy, your ultimate ruin is certain. But if you are one of God's people, your ultimate triumph is certain.

THE BLOODY CITY RUINED BUT WITHOUT COMFORT (vs.1-7)

The verse begins with an interjection. It is usually an expression of lamentation. It points to judgment. It is used 50 times in the prophets, and it is here aimed at Nineveh.

Her Crimes Noted (vs.1)

Nineveh is identified by her crimes.

She is a bloody city.
She is a lying city.
She is a plundering city.

She kills. She deceives. She steals. And she never gets enough.

Her Destruction Described (vs.2-3)

Once again, the Lord describes the city's ruin in the most vivid terms. They are visual terms and auditory terms.

The sound of the whip
The sound of the quaking (rumbling) wheel
The dashing of the horse
The skipping of the chariot
Horsemen charging
Swords and spears flashing in the sunlight or moonlight
The dead are innumerable

Her Character Noted (vs.4)

A spiritual prostitute
A deadly charmer
A disloyal prostitute
A destructive charmer

Anyone who counts her an ally, anyone who believes the terms she offers, anyone who trusts her as a protector, is her prey.

Her Doom Announced (vs.5-7)

This is personal (vs.5a)
This is exposing (vs.5b)
This is contemptuous (vs.6)
This is complete and without pity (vs.7)

THE PROUD CITY HIDING BUT WITHOUT SAFETY (vs.8-11)

Would Nineveh think that it cannot happen to her? Would she rehearse in her mind all of her defenses, all her preparations, all her strengths, and all of her allies? No doubt, when you are the most powerful nation on the planet, predictions of your destruction seem very unreal to you. The proud don't feel vulnerable.

Maybe the people of God would think about those things too. Maybe the enemy of God's people seems too strong to be conquered. Maybe the promises of deliverance seem as unreal to them as the promises of destruction seem to Nineveh.

So, what does God do? He reminds them of another city that seemed too strong to be conquered. God reminds them of Thebes. Thebes, or No-Amon, had seemed to be totally defended as well. Yet, it was Assyria who conquered that Egyptian city.

The indestructible city that was destroyed by Assyria should speak to Assyria and to Judah about the fact that Nineveh can be destroyed, too. And God says that she *will be destroyed.* She will seek for refuge, she will look for help, but she won't find a hiding place or anyone who can deliver her.

THE HELPLESS CITY WOUNDED BUT WITHOUT SYMPATHY (vs.12-19)

She will prove, in fact, to be a helpless city. She imagines herself to be undefeatable, but God describes her as fruit ready to be eaten. She does not understand her vulnerability. When God exposes you to your enemies, you are not safe.

Her Many Fortresses Will be Devoured (vs.12)
Her Strong Troops Will Prove to be Weak (vs.13a)
Her Gates are Open (Their Bars are Burned) (vs.13b)
Her Efforts and Assets Will Prove Worthless (vs.14-18)

Preparations are worthless (vs.14-15)
Multiplication of forces are worthless (vs.15)
Multiplication of wealth and allies will prove worthless (vs.16)
Strength in leadership will prove worthless (vs.17-18)

Her Demise Will be Celebrated (vs.19)

Her crimes have been listed. Her punishments have been described. It is all so very simple and straightforward. God's enemies, the enemies of His people, will be judged. God's people will be delivered and vindicated.

Let the enemies of God fear. Let the friends of God live in hope. The true God is not only a God of mercy, He is a God of vengeance and jealousy and wrath—and He is holy in all of it. He is holy in every way. The destinies of men hinge on what their relationship is to this God. The destinies of nations hinge on how they are relating to this true God.

6
STUDY GUIDE

LESSON ONE

Text: Nahum (Overview)
Title: Meet The True God

Reading to Prepare:
Read the entire book of Nahum in one sitting.
Acts 17:19-23
Exodus 34:6-7
Proverbs 3:7
Hebrews 11:6
Revelation 21:1-8

INTRODUCTION:

What is unique about the form of Nahum?

What is unique about its historical context?

What are some of the unique contrasts found in the book?

What are some of the unique theological emphases in Nahum?

THE BOOK OF NAHUM TEACHES US THAT OUR CONCEPTION OF GOD IS OFTEN FAR TOO WEAK

Are you every ashamed of the wrath of God?

Do you fully acknowledge God's hatred for sin when you think about your own life?

THE BOOK OF NAHUM TEACHES US THAT OUR CONCEPTION OF GOD IS OFTEN FAR TOO SMALL

Do you think that your view of God does justice to His sovereignty over all human existence, including all human history?

Do you think that your view of God does justice to His sovereignty over the circumstances of your own daily life?

THE BOOK OF NAHUM TEACHES US THAT OUR CONCEPTION OF GOD IS OFTEN FAR TOO UNTRUSTING

Are you bothered by what you see happening in the world, so that you find yourself wondering why God hasn't changed things?

Do you believe that regardless of what things look like at the moment, God is a rewarder of those who trust Him?

LESSON TWO

Text: Nahum 1:1-8
Title: The God Who Determines All Things

Reading to Prepare:
Read Nahum 1:1-8 three times prior to the study.
1 Corinthians 3:16-17
Psalm 7:1-17

INTRODUCTION:

Explain how everything in the life of a person, or in the lives of groups of people (nations) will ultimately be determined by a relationship to God.

THE BURDENED PROPHET (vs.1)

Explain the meaning of the word "oracle" (ESV). In what sense was a prophet's message a burden?

What do we know about Nahum from the Bible?

What does the threefold description of the book (an oracle, a book, a vision) tell us about Nahum's message?

THE AWESOME GOD (vs.2-8)

What do these verses teach us about God's character and nature? There are six attributes listed in the text, what are they?
1.
2.
3.
4.
5.
6.

List some ways that each of these attributes encourage your worship of God.

What do these verses teach us about what God will and will not do?

List some ways that what God will and will not do, encourages your worship of God.

LESSON THREE

Text: Nahum 1:9-15
Title: Wrath or Refuge?

Reading to Prepare:
Read Nahum 1:9-15 three times prior to the study.
2 Kings 19:10-19, 32-37
Revelation 20:12-15
Romans 10:13-15

INTRODUCTION:

The background for these verses was covered in the previous chapter. To review, write a brief summary that explains what you know to be true because of who God reveals Himself to be, and what God reveals He will and will not do, in verses 1-8.

THE FUTILITY OF ASSYRIAN PLANS (vs.9-11)

The Assyrian plots against the city of Jerusalem are answered by God in three ways. List them here.

1. (vs.9) Your plans _____
2. (vs.10) Your future _____
3. (vs.11) Your counsels _____

What do you think becomes of your plans that do not reflect submission to God and His will?

THE END OF JUDAH'S OPPRESSION (vs.12-13)

In these verses, God acknowledges three present realities but promises three very different realities in the end. List those three contrasts.

1.
2.
3.

THE DEATH SENTENCE FOR ASSYRIA (vs.14)

What is the difference between a command from God that represents His prescriptive will, and a command that represents His decretive will?

Write a summary of what God decrees concerning Nineveh in this verse.

THE CALL FOR JUDAH'S WORSHIP (vs.15)

What does God's judgment upon the wicked mean for God's people?

How do these truths about our sovereign God change your worldview?

LESSON FOUR

Text: Nahum 2:1-13
Title: Destruction Declared

Reading to Prepare:
Read Nahum 2:1-13 three times prior to the study.
Isaiah 46:1-11
Hosea 14:1-7
Romans 8:31
Revelation 19:1-3
Revelation 22:1-5

INTRODUCTION:

Write your reflection on the following statement: The true and living God is not held captive by the future; He determines the future.

Name some of the attributes of God that make prophecy concerning future events possible.

What are some events, still future, that the Bible gives us information about?

THE SOUND OF DESTRUCTION (vs.1-2)

God calls the city of Nineveh to prepare for the destructive forces that He will send upon them. What does that teach you about God?

According to verse 2, what cause is God defending in the judgment that He will bring upon Nineveh?

THE SCENE OF DESTRUCTION (vs.3-10)

What did you think of the battle scene presented by Nahum, and what are some reasons why Yahweh would have given such detail?

THE SOBRIETY OF DESTRUCTION (vs.11-12)

The Lord mockingly describes what once characterized the lion, and then suggests that the lion cannot be found. What is the significance of this?

THE SURENESS OF DESTRUCTION (vs.13)

It is the unique glory of the living God to declare the end from the beginning. In Revelation 19 and 22 the Lord describes two different things that will last forever. What are these two things, and how do they speak to you?

LESSON FIVE

Text: Nahum 3:1-19
Title: Crimes and Punishment

Reading to Prepare:
Read Nahum 3:1-19 three times prior to the study.

INTRODUCTION:

The message of Nahum is simple but powerful. Do you think that we sometimes miss the Bible's powerful message by desiring something different than the simple straightforward lessons it presents? Explain.

THE BLOODY CITY RUINED BUT WITHOUT COMFORT (vs.1-7)

In the first verse, Nineveh's crimes are noted. Which crimes are specified?
1.
2.
3.

In verses 2-3, Nineveh's destruction is described in both visual and auditory terms. Which of these were striking to you and why? How do you think the original audience would have read these?

In verse 4, Nineveh's character is described. How is her character described and what is the significance of the description?

In verses 5-7, Nineveh's doom is announced. What stands out to you about this announcement?

THE PROUD CITY HIDING BUT WITHOUT SAFETY (vs.8-11)

Why do you think that God would remind Nineveh of the destruction of Thebes, but do so in a proclamation to His own people?

Is it possible that just like destruction doesn't seem real to the self-confident proud people who are headed for judgment, the destruction of the proud doesn't always seem possible to the people of God being oppressed or threatened by them? Explain.

THE HELPLESS CITY WOUNDED BUT WITHOUT SYMPATHY (vs.12-19)

Nineveh imagines itself to be indestructible. God describes the city like fruit ready to be devoured. Briefly summarize how God described the city's demise (before it had actually occurred), and any lessons that are imparted to your life as a result.

ABOUT THE AUTHOR

Richard Caldwell Jr. is the senior pastor at Founders Baptist Church in Spring, Texas. He has served in pastoral ministry since 1984. He and his wife Jacquelyn have been married for 34 years and give joyful thanks for their children and grandchildren. Richard is a graduate of Southwestern Baptist Theological Seminary (M.Div.) and The Master's Seminary (D.Min.). He serves as the campus pastor for the Expositor's Seminary's Houston campus. Walking in Grace Media Ministries is the preaching and print ministry of pastor Caldwell.

Made in United States
North Haven, CT
12 November 2022

26556820R00030